TEXAS NIGHT BEFORE CHRISTMAS
COLORING BOOK

Written and Illustrated by JAMES RICE

Pelican Publishing Company
GRETNA 1989

ISBN: 0-88289-727-6

First printing

Manufactured in the United States of America

Published by Pelican Publishing Company
1101 Monroe Street, Gretna, Louisiana 70053

'Twas the night before Christmas

A blue Texas norther
roared over the plains.

The cold fairly whistled
through the loose winderpanes.

I poked at the farplace
to stir up a flame.

Ma fixed up our dinner
to be ready next day.

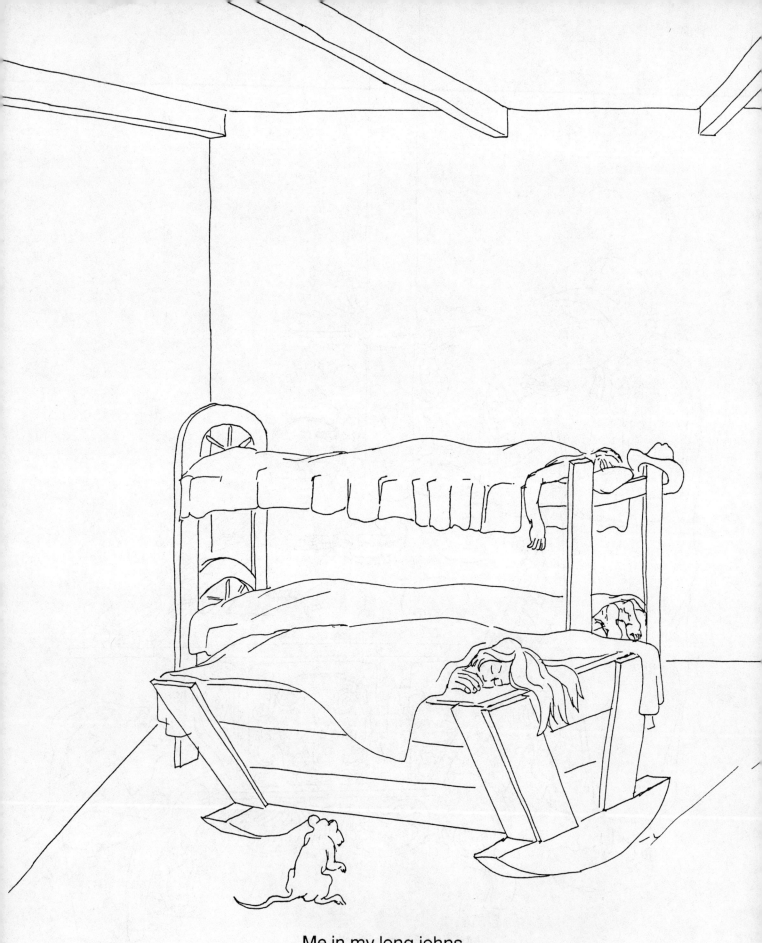

Me in my long johns
and Ma in her gown

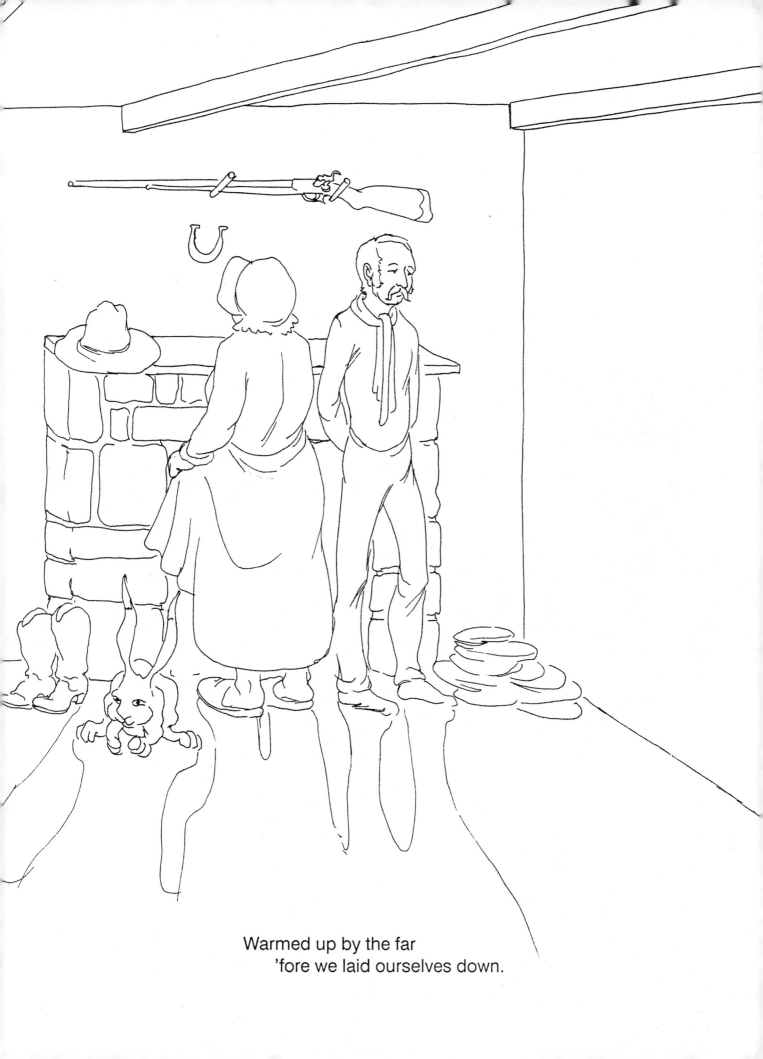

Warmed up by the far
'fore we laid ourselves down.

The young'uns were bundled
down snug in their covers.

Then from out on the range
there came such a ruckus.

There were eight scroungy longhorns
stampedin' around

In front of a wagon
piled high as could be.

Their longhorn head honcho
was old Santy Claus!

He got their attention
and called them by name.

"Git on, Sam and High-Hips,
let's move this here wagon!"

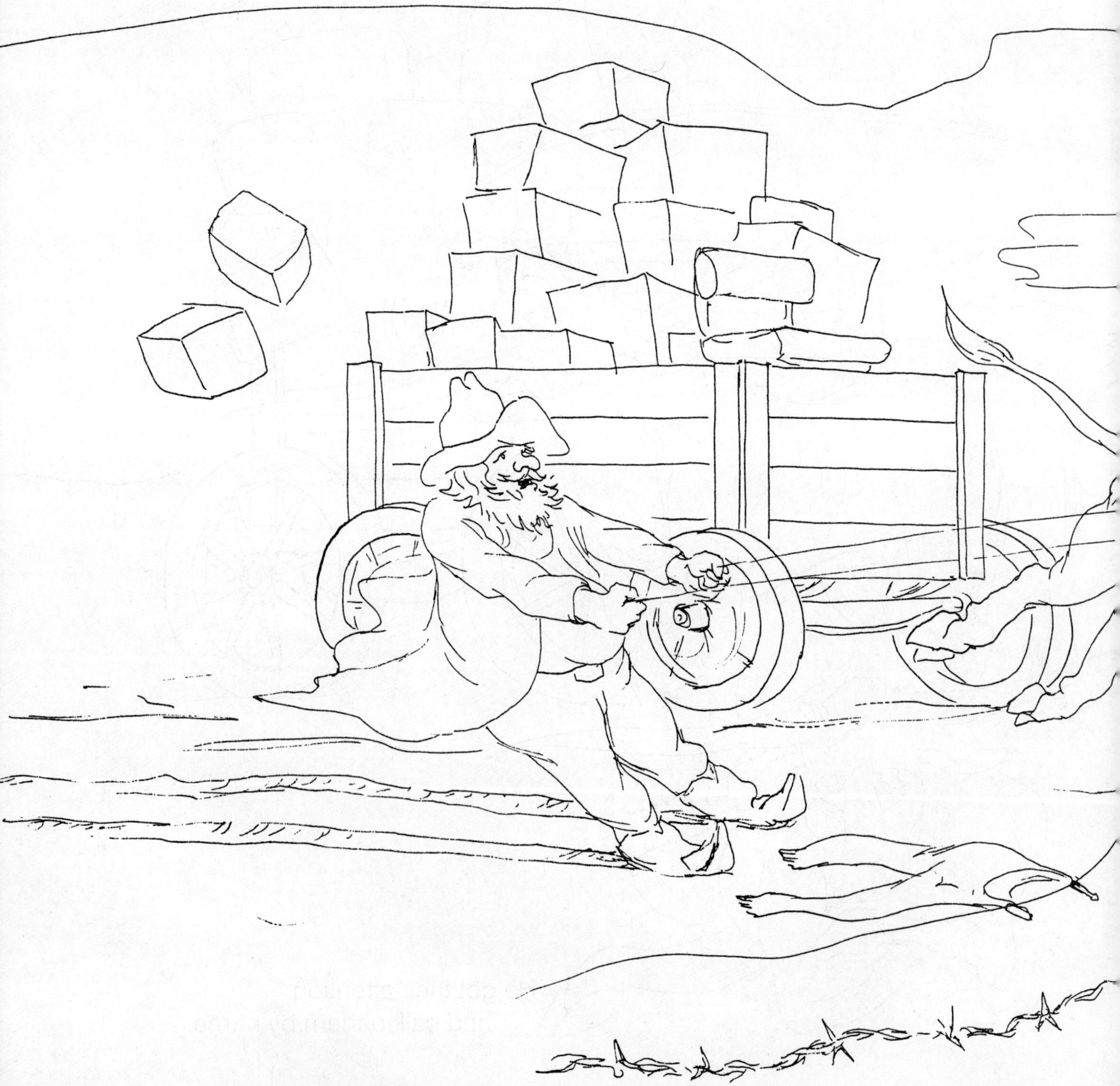

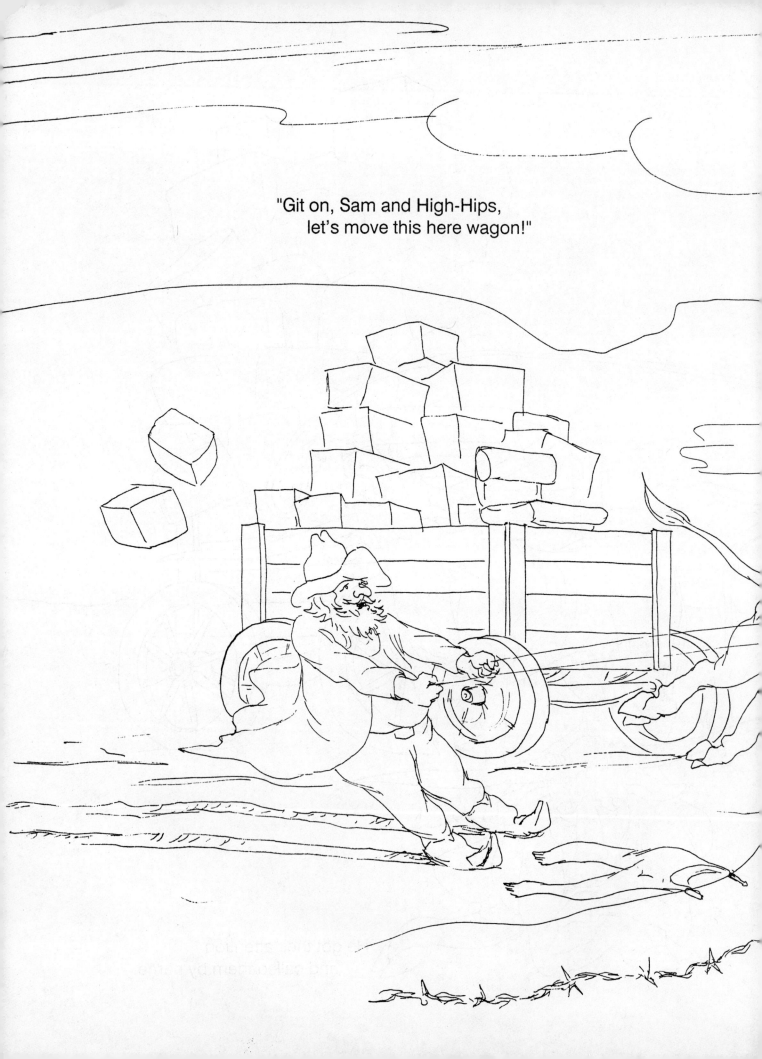

Then straight on they trampled
through Ma's flower bed.

They laid the gate flat,
    and the clothesline went, too.

Santy pulled them up short
on top of the roof.

They rocked our sod shanty,
   the dirt sifted down.

And then through the chimney
Santy came with a bound!

He was dressed all in rawhide
with a Stetson on top.

A feed bag of toys
he flung from his back.

He filled all the boots
and piled them up high.

The cold Texas norther
still whistled and blew.

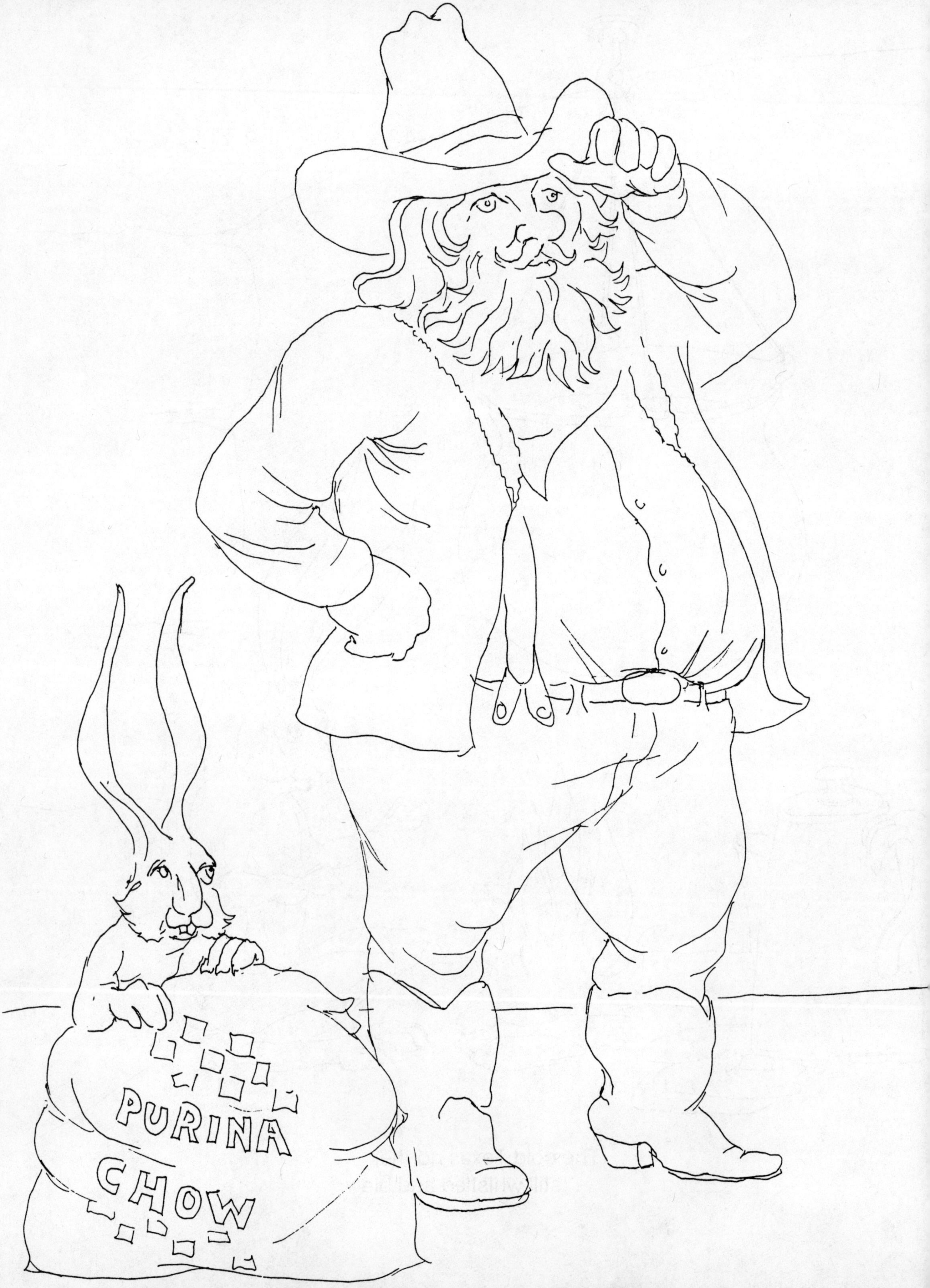
PURINA
CHOW

He looked out the winder
and up at the sky.

More young'uns was waitin'—
his work wasn't through.

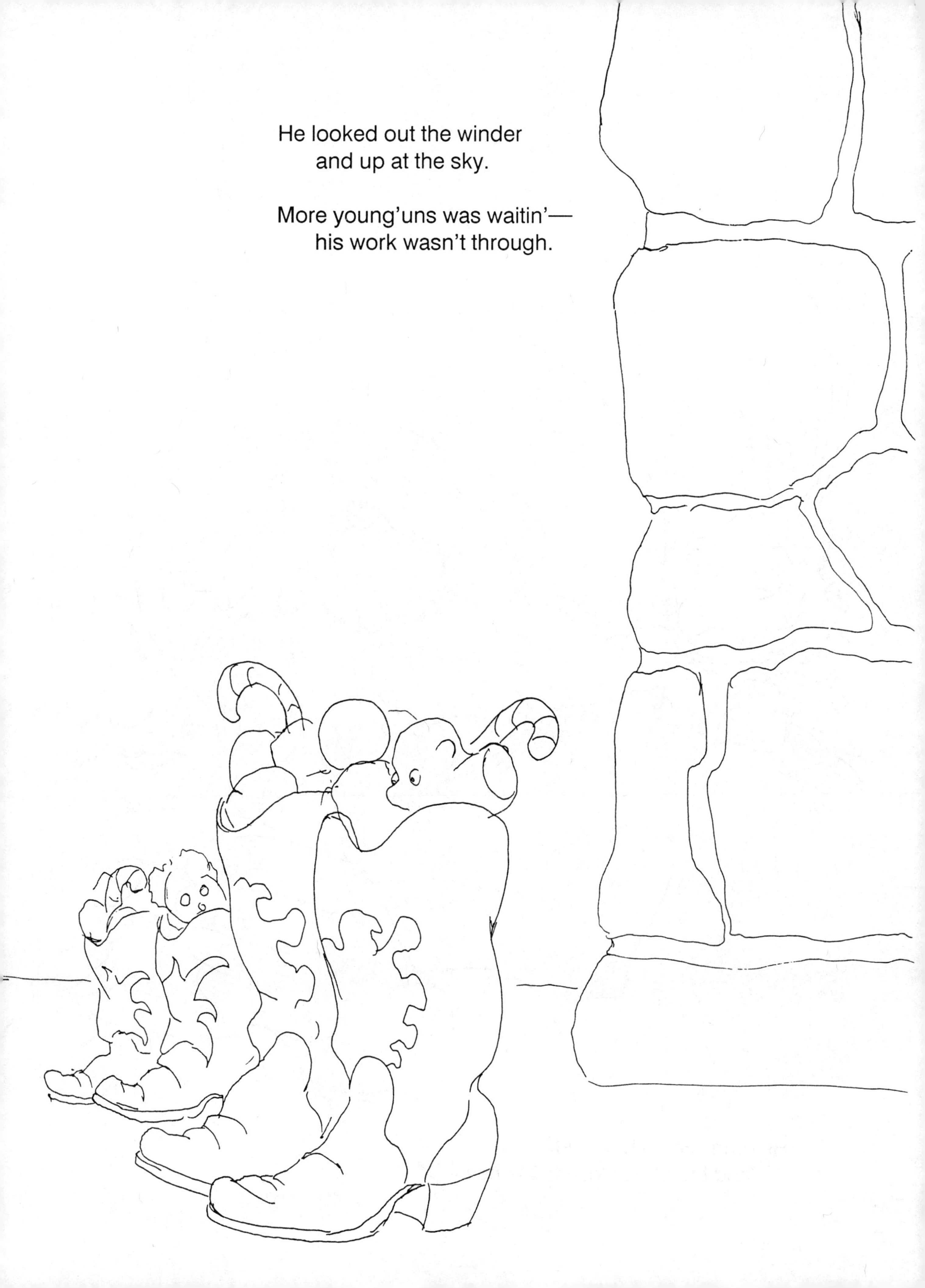

He drank some hot mud
   and hunched close to the heat

To soak up the warmth
and thaw his cold feet.

He prodded the longhorns
to get on the go,

And the wagon took off
through the fog and the snow.

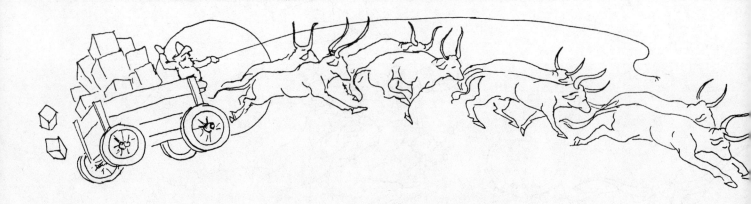

"Merry Christmas, y'heah?
And y'all have a good night!"